Moondust and Mystery

Magic Poems

chosen by John Foster

illustrated by Peter Bailey

Contents

Before

Before mountains found their place
and raindrops knew their way.

Before questions had an answer
and children ran to play.

Before oceans knew their name
and sunshine filled each dawn.

Before the world began to spin,
Magic was born.

Andrew Collett

Witching Woman's Riddle

My first's in the moon
But not in the stars.

My second is kept
Bottled up in a jar.

My third is a gift
That you'll find in the ground.

My fourth you will sing
If you dance in a ring
Bearing ivy and incense
As you twist round and round.

My last creeps in with the black cat
And brings an end to logic.

My riddle's a spell:
The answer is . . .

David Greygoose

(MAGIC)

Enter the World of Enchantment

Enter the world of Enchantment,
Step through the silver gate
To the land where sprites and fairies,
Hags and mermaids wait.
Explore the soaring mountains,
Lakes and forests deep,
Stormy seas and snowscapes,
A haunted castle keep.

Enter the world of Enchantment,
Step through the arch of gold
To the land where spells are made
And ancient tales are told.
Bring courage in your heart
For there are dangers here to brave:
Sorcerers and serpents,
Fiery dragons in their caves.

Enter the world of Enchantment,
Step through the mirror glass
To a land that holds you spellbound
As wraiths and goblins pass.
Sing with feasting elves,
Dance where the demons fly,
Enter the world of Enchantment
Before the chance slips by . . .

Gill Davies

The Wizard

He came from the west
Of the setting sun
From the Islands of Mystery,
And he stood on the cliff-top gazing out
At the restless, roaring sea.

His fingertips flashed
With magical sparks
As he opened his book of charms,
And raised his ancient staff in the air
And ordered the waves to be calm.

He conjured dragons
Who breathed out flames
From shadowy deep-sea caves,
And golden eagles flew at his call
Across the rippling waves.

Glistening mermaids
Heard his soft voice
And swam from the deep sea-bed,
And unicorns galloped across the sands
Tossing their silvery heads.

And those who saw
These wonderful sights
Say that when all this was done,
The wizard returned to his island home
To the west of the setting sun.

But still they talk
Of the day he came
From the Islands of Mystery,
And how his power was as wide and deep
As the sparkling dream-filled sea.

Cynthia Rider

Come In!

This is the wizard's hidey-hole,
hidey-hole, hidey-hole.
This is the wizard's hidey-hole.
Be careful where you tread.

Don't step on that toad,
don't slip on that eel,
and if a bat lands on your head
—don't squeal!

You may sniff at his potions
and give them a stir,
say '*good day*' to his cat
and tickle her fur.

You may try on his hat,
you may play with his mice,
but don't ever, ever
    touch his wand
or you'll v-a-n-i-s-h
    —in a trice!

Patricia Leighton

The Miserable Wizard of Misery Hall

The miserable wizard of Misery Hall
doesn't like children, no, not at all.
In fact schoolchildren quite often pass by his door
and finish the trip not on two legs but four,
changed into hamsters and stripy green rats,
shocking pink gerbils, and polka-dot cats.
Parents complain, but their teachers don't mind.
Small creatures are not so much trouble they find,
and are sending the rest of their pupils to call
on the miserable wizard of Misery Hall.

Marian Swinger

Blizzard

I'm Blizzard, a wizard
Of wretched endeavour,
My whims are my own,
And I do as I choose.
I trifle with humans
For simple amusement,
I plague them with hiccups
While shrinking their shoes.

I'm Blizzard, a wizard
Of peevish demeanour,
I'm crabby, I'm cranky,
I'm crusty, I'm cross.
A wave of my wand,
You're a tree in a forest,
A blink of my eye,
And you're covered in moss.

I'm Blizzard, a wizard
Of woeful employments,
My methods are many,
My ways are bizarre.
One snap of my fingers,
You're dripping with syrup,
One twitch of my nostrils,
You're slathered with tar.

I'm Blizzard, a wizard
Of hostile intention,
I'll turn you to tallow,
To jelly, to clay—
Your presence annoys me,
You're ever unwelcome,
I'm Blizzard the wizard,
Stay out of my way!

Jack Prelutsky

Invisible Wizard's Regret

I'm in a preposterous pickle,
My prospects appear to be black.
I witlessly made myself vanish,
And now I can't get myself back.

Jack Prelutsky

Advice to Young Wizards

Unicorns are born
with *tiny* horns,
even dragons
have to learn
how to breathe flame;

so don't blame
me, if your first spell
doesn't bring you fame,
by turning lead to gold.

Merlin wasn't always
quite so old
or quite so wise;
take my advice,
aim for something
less likely to make
mistakes,
like changing water into ice.

Slip cubes into your
slugslime-and-frogspawn-shake;
relax.
      Try another slice
of goblin cake.
Keep cool,
take things easy and you'll
love your years
at wizard school.

Mike Johnson

Wizard Witter World

I've got the *Wizard Witter* hat and cloak,
with *Wizard Witter* wand,
Wizard Witter wallpaper,
Wizard Witter duvet and pillow,
matching *Wizard Witter* curtains,
and *Wizard Witter* waste bin and bedside lamp.

Wizard Witter's cat, owl, and scary monster
grin from the window sill.
Wizard Witter and the Withered Watchstrap
and all the other Wizard Witter books
are on my bookshelf—
but I've not read them yet.

I eat my *Wizard Witter* wheat flakes
from my *Wizard Witter* bowl
with my *Wizard Witter* spoon
and wipe my mouth with
my *Wizard Witter* serviette.

I pack my *Wizard Witter* lunch box
with my *Wizard Witter* snacks
from the fridge covered in
Wizard Witter magnets.

Then off to school
in my *Wizard Witter* anorak
carrying my *Wizard Witter* backpack.

Here come my mates Pooky and Pongo
in their *Wiz–* Uhh?
In their **MAGIMONSTER** trainers and
MAGIMONSTER baseball caps!

'You're not still into Wizard Witter, are you?'
says Pooky, turning her cap back to front.

Rita Ray

Lost Magic

'Chuckles the Magician'
Isn't laughing any more,
He's got a new 'half-sister'—
And he blames it on his saw . . .
For his hands ARE rather shaky
And he suffers from bad health.
(His eyesight's so appalling,
He's just hypnotized himself!)

He now looks old and wrinkled,
And his life is filled with cares.
From hats, he once pulled rabbits—
But now it's only hairs.
So he needs a 'perfect exit'—
And he's placing all his hope
In trying hard to 'vanish'
Up his piece of Indian rope . . . !

Trevor Harvey

The Wonderful Hat

'My wonderful hat,' the magician said,
'contains much more than just my head.
To list what's in it would take hours,
but first, I shall produce some flowers,
and here's a rabbit, alive and kicking,
and a baby hippo; oh, it's sticking.
Now a hundred hankies tied together,
twenty mice, and an ostrich feather,
and here's the ostrich, mind those legs,
followed by two dragon's eggs.
The mother dragon must be vexed.
I rather hope she won't be next.'
He reached inside; out came a gannet
and after that, a tiny planet.
'Bother,' the magician said,
'it's orbiting around my head.'
He threw the hat upon the floor,
then, from its depths, a dragon roared.
'Oops!' he said. 'Well, mustn't stop,'
and vanished with a little pop.
The audience fled with twinkling legs
as the dragon snarled, 'Where are my eggs?'

Marian Swinger

Riddle

Can you find the letters here
Which spell my name and spread great fear?
Have a go, try your best,
Solve the riddle, pass the test.

My first is in **danger** and **demon**, that's me,
My second's in **fire** which I breathe fiercely,
My third hides in **scales** which cover my back,
And my fourth lies in **gold** which I guard from attack,
My fifth is in **smoke** which I blow out in rings,
Whilst my last is in **talons** and also in **wings**.

Richard Caley

The Dragon's Curse

Enter darkness. Leave the light.
Here be nightmare. Here be fright.
Here be dragon, flame, and flight.
Here be spit-fire. Here be grief.
So curse the bones of unbelief.
Curse the creeping treasure-thief.
Curse much worse the dragon-slayer.
Curse his purse and curse his payer.
Curse these words. Preserve their sayer.
Earth and water, fire and air.
Prepare to meet a creature rare.
Enter, now, if you dare.
Enter, now . . . the dragon's lair!

Nick Toczek

Dragons' Wood

We didn't see dragons
in Dragons' Wood
but we saw
where the dragons had been.

We saw tracks in soft mud
that could only have been scratched
by some sharp-clawed creature.

We saw scorched earth
where fiery dragon breath
had whitened everything to ash.

We saw trees burnt to charcoal.
We saw dragon dung
rolled into boulders.

And draped from a branch
we saw sloughed off skin,
scaly, still warm . . .

We didn't see dragons
in Dragons' Wood,
but this was the closest
we'd ever been

to believing.

Brian Moses

Waiting

Down underground, two days' climb deep,
there the dragon lies asleep.
Curled waiting where the rocks keep warm
his ancient, armoured, reptile form—
no match, now magic is no more,
for knights and swords and guns of war.
Through countless spans of sun and moon,
he's hidden in these catacombs.

Down underground, two days' climb deep,
each thousand years he wakes from sleep,
and lumbers, scales rasping, eyes aglow,
with fire and lava from below,
to sniff and taste and test the air—
each time detecting more hope there.
Then slowly turns without regret.
He can wait. It's not time.
Yet.

Liz Brownlee

· ·. .·* * ✳ 25

Mama-Wata

Down by the seaside
when the moon is in bloom
sits Mama-Wata
gazing up at the moon

She sits as she combs
her hair like a loom
she sits as she croons
a sweet kind of tune

But don't go near Mama-Wata
when the moon is in bloom
for sure she will take you
down to your doom.

Grace Nichols

Sailor's Warning

Over the sound of the surging seas
And the whistling wild wind's whip
Beware the sound of a siren's song
That will seal the fate of a ship.

For the siren's song is a mermaid's song
With a haunting magical note
It's heard at the height of a raging storm
And is sure to wreck your boat.

Beware the sound of the mermaid's song
As she combs her golden hair
For the mermaid's song is a dangerous song
And sailors must take care.

For the mermaid's song from the jagged rocks
Lures sailors far and wide
For the mermaid's song is a siren's song
Sending ships beneath the tide.

So, if over the sound of the surging seas
And the whistling wild wind's whip
You follow the sound of a mermaid's song
You will surely sink your ship.

Brenda Williams

Sea Dream

I dreamt I was a mermaid
    with a turbo-tail,
Racing through the water
    with a twin-jet whale.
A supersonic octopus
    and mega-mouth squid
Chased us to a shipwreck
    where a skeleton hid.

When I woke up in the morning
    I had seaweed on my head,
Gold coins and precious pearls
    were scattered on my bed.
I brushed the sand from every pearl.
    I gathered up the treasure.
I counted up the gold coins
    and beat my tail with pleasure.

Celia Warren

To Speak a Spell

Catch a star
In the lake.
Say, 'Aha!'
Take a rake
Fish it out
Hang it high.
There's no doubt
By and by
It will shine
With a glow
Green and fine.
You will know
It's the time
To cast a spell.
Speak in rhyme
And never tell.

Jenny Morris

Hokum Pokum

Hokum pokum
Dog's old bone
Let all teachers
Turn to stone.

Hokum pokum
Black cat's paw
Stay like that
For evermore.

Clive Webster

Spells'R'Us

Come along to see us
If you're looking for a spell;
Spells and magic potions
Are what we have to sell.

Want to buy a broomstick?
We've got a fabulous range;
We'll even take your old one,
Only we do part-exchange.

Want a spell to change people
Into newts or frogs or toads?
C'mon down to Spells'R'Us
We've got loads and loads!

Want to be able to make
Yourself just up and disappear?
Why not try 'Invisible Me'
Just voted 'Spell of the Year'.

We've Spell Books for Beginners
And volumes for the More Advanced;
Mystical tomes full of secrets
Which'll leave you quite entranced.

We've wands and we've magic rings
And traditional wizard hats;
Owls who tuwhit-tuwhoo on cue
And well-trained pure black cats!

Come along to Spells'R'Us
If you want to find a spell;
Spells and magic potions
Are what we have to sell.

Tony Langham

The Witch's Shopping List

Pound of pickled porcupine,
Slug slime spread,
Three ripe bull-frogs,
One rat (dead).
Large tin of termites,
Small bag of flies,
Alligator muesli
(Economy size).
Rags to the laundry,
Skunk shampoo,
Pick up pension,
That's it. Phew!

Kaye Umansky

Midsummer Magic

There's magic in the air tonight
As under the starry sky
A whisper of mischievous fairy folk
Tiptoe merrily by.

There's magic in the air tonight
As from the deep sea-caves
A shimmer of silvery mermaids
Swim through the lacy waves.

There's magic in the air tonight
As under the rustling trees
A glimmer of golden unicorns
Toss their heads in the breeze.

There's magic in the air tonight
As from the moon's pale beams
A sprinkle of midsummer magic
Falls gently onto your dreams.

Cynthia Rider

Midsummer Night

Madness, my nan says.
But I want to go out in the dark
looking for fairies. I'm sure they'd
come when I call or if I tiptoe

I might just catch them at their revels
dancing in a ring. I know where
the ring is. Grandad told me
to watch where bluebells grow.

Angela Topping

The Darkling Elves

In wildest woods, on treetop shelves,
sit evil beings with evil selves—
they are the dreaded darkling elves
and they are always hungry.

In garish garb of capes and hoods,
they wait and watch within their woods
to peel your flesh and steal your goods
for they are always hungry.

Through brightest days and darkest nights
these terrifying tiny sprites
await to strike and take their bites
for they are always hungry.

Watch every leaf of every tree,
for once they pounce you cannot flee—
their teeth are sharp as sharp can be . . .
and they are always hungry.

Jack Prelutsky

Thomas the Troll

Here comes Thomas
the big bad troll,
head of rock
and eyes like coals,
body of granite,
marble legs,
arms of flint
and teeth like pegs.
His brain's the size
of a small, green pea,
but he's the size
of a medium tree.
He loves rock music
and likes to munch
tasty boulders
for his lunch.
But if you see him
acting tough,
just mention good
old Billy Goat Gruff.

Marian Swinger

Trick or Treat

Trick or treat, trick or treat
Pumpkins light up every street
Trick or treat, trick or treat
Witches watch and gremlins greet
Trick or treat, trick or treat
Skeletons and vampires meet
Trick or treat or trick or treat.

Hallowe'en, Hallowe'en
Ghosts and ghouls glowing green
Hallowe'en, Hallowe'en
Werewolves, hairy, scary, mean
Hallowe'en, Hallowe'en
Mummies lurch and monsters lean
Hallo Hallo Hallowe'en.

Paul Cookson

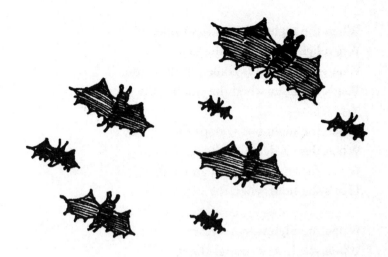

Tonight's the Night!

I don't want to go out tonight, Mum,
I don't want to go out tonight
There's a whistling wind and a cold yellow moon,
And shadows dance eerily out in the gloom,
I'd like to stay in my own little room.
I don't want to go out tonight.

But you must go out tonight, my dear,
It's the night when you have to be seen.
So put on your cloak and pick up the black cat,
Find your charms and your spells and your long
    pointed hat,
And get on to your broomstick and fly like a bat,
You're a witch and tonight's Hallowe'en!

Gervase Phinn

The Hour When the Witches Fly

When the night is as cold as stone,
When lightning severs the sky,
When your blood is chilled to the bone,
That's the hour when the witches fly.

When the night-owl swoops for the kill,
When there's death in the fox's eye,
When the snake is coiled and still,
That's the hour when the witches fly.

When the nightmares scream in your head,
When you hear a strangled cry,
When you startle awake in your bed,
That's the hour when the witches fly.

When the sweat collects on your brow,
When the minutes tick slowly by,
When you wish it was then not now,
That's the hour when the witches fly.

John Foster

The Babysitter

I knew she was different the moment she arrived
And parked her broomstick neatly in our porch.

Her cat pranced in as if he owned the place
And mine shot out as if he'd seen a ghost.

When I asked her if she'd like a cup of tea
She said 'No, bat-juice would be nice.'

She told the best bedtime stories in the world
But on my cheek her goodnight kiss fell cold as ice.

Frances Nagle

Which Witch?

Witches are all shapes and sizes;
Many of them wear disguises.
So it's very hard to spot
Which is a witch and which is not.

Marcus Parry

Two Witches Discuss Good Grooming

'How do you keep your teeth so green
Whilst mine remain quite white?
Although I rub them vigorously
With cold slime every night.

'Your eyes are such a lovely shade
Of bloodshot, streaked with puce.
I prod mine daily with a stick
But it isn't any use.

'I envy so, the spots and boils
That brighten your complexion.
Even rat spit on my face
Left no trace of infection.

'I've even failed to have bad breath
After eating sewage raw,
Yet your halitosis
Can strip paint from a door.'

*'My dear, there is no secret,
Now I don't mean to brag.
What you see is nature's work
I'm just a natural hag.'*

John Coldwell

Miss More

There's something strange about Miss More,
(she's come to live at number four),
she has a cloak behind the door,
and a broomstick in the corner.

She's tall and thin and rather flat,
she stares at me—not only that—
she hangs a most peculiar hat
with that broomstick in the corner.

She makes stuff in an iron pot,
and late at night she's out a lot,
I often wonder why she's got
that broomstick in the corner.

I think I'll call on Hallowe'en,
and try and find out where she's been.
It's time she knew that someone's seen,
that broomstick in the corner.

Linda Allen

The Witches' Under-World Cup Final

Report:
The Final of the Witches' Under-World Cup
Was played at Trembly Stadium
On October 31st, naturally!

The finalists were Northwitch Crawlers,
Who had beaten WereWolves in the semis
And Eastwitch Flyers who won their semi
Against Aston Villains.

Both teams wore their away strip—
Black vertical stripes on a black background.
The game was recorded for *Witch of the Day*.

The referee was Mr Crombie a local Zombie,
Who warned the teams to play dirty,
And not to indulge in any ladylike behaviour.

A black cat was tossed into the air,
To start the game
And it came down tails,
So, as it was their cat, Eastwitch kicked off.

During the match
The Eastwitch striker was struck by lightning,
Their sweeper lost her broomstick,
And one of their wingers was sent off—
For low-flying.

The Northwitch ghoulie was shown a blood-red card
For kicking the referee—
Into touch.
One of their hump-backs went off for a spell—
And hasn't been seen since.

A spooksman said the match had to be abandoned,
Because there was trouble brewing,
And anyway—
It was getting light!

David Whitehead

Wicked Winter Tree

Beware the wicked winter tree
when it twists its twilight spell:
when it tangles itself into witches' hair,
black and bleak as a bottomless well,
and scrapes the sunset bare.

Watch out for the wicked winter tree
when it sweeps up the evening sky,
for who can tell what sneaky spell
may linger there, in its witches' hair,
waiting for a passer-by?

Kate Williams

✻❋ ✳✳ ✲

Wishing Well

There's a well at the bottom of the garden,
A cavernous, deep abyss,
And it's said that if you throw a coin,
You can make a wish.

But there also have been rumours
Of those who disappear,
When they toss a penny
And dare to get too near.

They say the well is waiting
For some unwary soul
To lean too far and find themselves
Falling down that hole!

So do not then be tempted
To stand up on your toes,
When you throw some money
And look for where it goes.

Because you could lose your balance—
Disappear from view—
Tumbling
    headlong
        down
           that
              well
Could be the end of you!!

Anne Logan

The Forest of No Return

Where have the knights gone
And where is the king?

> They rode out to drink
> From the magic spring.

What did they find
In the forest so wild?

> A hunt and a hare
> And a fairy child.

When will the king
Return with his men?
When shall we see them?

> Never again.

Sue Cowling

On Reflection

Don't practise strange spells in front of the mirror,
don't point at yourself, with a wand;
don't practise strange spells in front of the mirror,
I did—now I live in this pond.

Mike Johnson

The Brown Bear

In the dark wood
In a clearing
Sleeps a brown bear
Dreaming, dreaming

His skin was furless
His paws were clawless
He walked into the city
Lawless, lawless

The moon was hidden
The clouds were weeping
A princess slumbered
Sleeping, sleeping

The thief climbed into
The royal bedroom
And stole her ruby
Heirloom, heirloom

The ruby glowed
With fire and lightning
A spell was cast
Frightening, frightening

The thief grew fur
His body thickened
His hands grew claws
He sickened, sickened

Beneath the black sky
Thunder rumbled
Into the dark wood
He stumbled, stumbled

In the ruby
Gleaming, gleaming
Dwells a wizard
Scheming, scheming

In the dark wood
In a clearing
Sleeps a brown bear
Dreaming, dreaming

Roger Stevens

Witchwater

Glimmering, shimmering down by the clearing
Under a shadowing tree
Witchwater's waiting to catch the uncaring
And nobody knows it but me
Green in the evening and blue afternoons
Silvery under the stars
Witchwater's beautiful, glowing and beckoning
Calling with dangerous charm

Enchanted and dreaming I'm here in the clearing
I wait by the shadowing tree
Centuries pass since I looked in the water
But time doesn't matter to me
Whoever you are and whatever you're seeking
Hurry away and be free
Don't look in the water—the fathomless water
Or you'll be a statue like me!

Sally Farrell Odgers

Troll

Under the bridge
   where the water flows
is a secret dwelling
   that no one knows—
dark and solemn
   the shadows stay,
with never a spark
   from the golden day.

Somebody told me
   once they saw
a slithery, slimy
   weed-wet door,
and the flick of a beard
   went in and out—
two bright, brown eyes
   and a turned-up snout.

Somebody whispered
   somebody said
a TROLL lives down on
   the river bed
and that's the place
   that he likes to be.

Somebody saw him . . .
    Was it me?

Jean Kenward

Once...

Long moons ago
in a silver dawn
around the time
when the stars were born
a beautiful horse
with a twisted horn
as smooth as silk
but sharp as a thorn
danced out of the mist
towards the sun . . .

and the dew-bright horse
with the twisted horn
that first danced then
when the stars were born
danced in the name of
unicorn,
long moons ago
in that new-world dawn.

Judith Nicholls

Unicorn

Where is the Unicorn?
Where did he go?
With his silver spike
And his mane of snow?

Deep in the secret world
Hidden from day,
He's only a whisper,
A heartbeat away.
Safe in a forest
No hunter can find . . .

But cover your eyes,
Keep watch with your mind,
Murmur a wish to the
Stars and the Moon,
And maybe you'll see him.
Some day. Very soon.

Where is the Unicorn?
Where did he go?
With his silver spike
And his mane of snow?

Clare Bevan

Pegasus

Tonight I woke from dreaming
And saw a shadow pass—
A horse swooped by my window
And now it pounds the grass.

His mane is pale as moonlight,
His silver feathers shine,
His tail streams like a comet,
And his starry eyes meet mine.

His mighty wings are beating,
So now I must decide
To hide my face in terror,
Or to trust my dreams . . .
    and RIDE!

Clare Bevan

Magic Carpet

Magic carpet,
your bright colours
delight the eye.

Your moons and stars
and midnight blues
sing of the sky.

Magic carpet,
kept in the cupboard,
I hear you sigh.

Let me unroll
your magic pattern
and help you fly.

Tony Mitton

Invisible Magicians

Thanks be to all magicians,
The ones we never see,
Who toil away both night and day
Weaving spells for you and me.

The ones who paint the rainbows
The ones who salt the seas
The ones who purify the dew
And freshen up the breeze.

The ones who brighten lightning
The ones who whiten snow
The ones who shine the sunshine
And give the moon its glow.

The ones who buff the fluffy clouds
And powder blue the skies
The ones who splash the colours on
The sunset and sunrise.

The ones who light volcanoes
The ones who soak the showers
The ones who wave the waves
And open up the flowers.

The ones who spring the spring
And warm the summer air
The ones who carpet autumn
And frost the winter earth.

The ones who polish icicles
The ones who scatter stars
The ones who cast their magic spells
Upon this world of ours.

Thanks to one and thanks to all,
Invisible and true,
Nature's magic heaven sent
To earth for me and you.

Paul Cookson

Jack Frost

Jack Frost,
Winter wizard
Brightens up the darkest night
Spells while we are fast asleep.

Jack Frost,
Winter jeweller
Encrusting spiders' webs with diamonds,
Icicle fingertips, silver breath.

Jack Frost,
Winter graffiti artist
Spray-can magic, leaves his mark,
Christmas card scenery, the icing on the lake.

Paul Cookson

Charm for Sweet Dreams

May the ghost
  lie in its grave.
May the Vampire
  see the light.
May the Witch
  keep to her cave.
May the Spectre
  melt from sight.

May the Wraith
  stay in the wood.
May the Banshee
  give no fright.
May the Ghoul
  be gone for good.
May the zombie
  haste its flight.

May the Troll
  no more be seen.
May the Werewolf
  lose its bite.
May all Spooks
  and Children Green
fade for ever
    in
        the
          night . . .

Wes Magee

Charm Bracelet

On my bracelet hangs:

The fold and flick of a fan,
The wink from a wishing well,

The dart of a bird's flight,
The curve in the shape of a bell,

The pearly gaze of the moon,
The click in the turn of a key,

The twitch on a cat's back,
The honey scent of a bee.

Fan, well, bird, bell,
Moon, key, cat, bee,

Bring good luck to me!

Mary Green

Gypsy Rosa

Tell my future, Gypsy Rosa,
Gaze into your crystal ball
Share the secrets of your magic
See my future, tell me all.
Will I ever slay a dragon
Will I meet a fair princess
Will I scale a mighty tower
Save a damsel in distress?
Will I find a mystic genie
Trapped inside a magic lamp
Like Aladdin in the story
In a cavern cold and damp?

In your dreams you'll slay a dragon
You will meet a fair princess
You will scale a mighty tower
Save a damsel in distress.
You will find a mystic genie
Trapped inside a magic lamp
Like Aladdin in the story
In a cavern cold and damp.
Do you have imagination?
Close your eyes and you will find
Everything you ever dreamed of
In the magic of your mind.

Granville Lawson

Index of titles/first lines

(First lines in italic)

ACKNOWLEDGEMENTS

We are grateful for permission to reproduce the following poems:

Linda Allen: 'Miss More', copyright © Linda Allen, first published in *Here Come the Heebie Jeebies*, compiled by Tony Bradman (Hodder, 2000), reprinted by permission of Rogers Coleridge & White; **John Coldwell:** 'Two Witches Discuss Good Grooming', first published in *HA–HA! 100 Poems To Make You Laugh*, edited by Paul Cookson (Macmillan, 2001), reprinted by permission of the author; **Paul Cookson:** 'Jack Frost' from *Very Best of Paul Cookson* (Macmillan, 2001), copyright © Paul Cookson 2001, reprinted by permission of the author; **Gill Davies:** 'Enter the World of Enchantment' from *Enchantment* (Brimax, 1999), reprinted by permission of the publisher; **John Foster:** 'The Hour When the Witches Fly' from *Four O'Clock Friday* (Oxford University Press, 1991), copyright © John Foster 1991, reprinted by permission of the author; **David Greygoose:** 'Witching Woman's Riddle' from *The Tree of Dreams* (Collins Educational, 1996), copyright © David Greygoose 1996, reprinted by permission of the author; **Mike Johnson:** 'On Reflection' first published in *Ye New Spell Book*, edited by Brian Moses (Macmillan, 2002), reprinted by permission of the author; **Wes Magee:** 'Charm for Sweet Dreams' from *The Phantom's Fang-tastic Show* (Oxford University Press, 2000), copyright © Wes Magee 2000, reprinted by permission of the author; **Tony Mitton:** 'Magic Carpet' from *Plum* (Scholastic Children's Books, 1998), copyright © Tony Mitton 1998, reprinted by permission of David Higham Associates Ltd; **Brian Moses:** 'Dragons' Wood' from *Barking Back at Dogs* (Macmillan, 2000), copyright © Brian Moses 2000, reprinted by permission of the author; **Grace Nichols:** 'Mama Wata', copyright © Grace Nichols 2002, first published in this collection by permission of Curtis Brown Ltd, London on behalf of the author; **Sally Farrell Odgers:** 'Witchwater' first published in *Petrifying Poems* compiled by Jane Covernton (Omnibus Books, 1986), reprinted by permission of the author; **Jack Prelutsky:** 'Invisible Wizard's Regret' and 'Blizzard' from *Monday's Troll* (Greenwillow Books, 1996), copyright © Jack Prelutsky 1996, reprinted by permission of HarperCollins Publishers Inc.; **Nick Toczek:** 'The Dragon's Curse' from *The Dragon Who Ate Our School* (Macmillan Children's Books, 1995), copyright © Nick Toczek 1995, reprinted by permission of the author; **Kaye Umansky:** 'The Witch's Shopping List' from *Witches In Stitches* (Puffin, 1988), reprinted by permission of the author; **Celia Warren:** 'Sea Dream' from *Fairground Toast & Buttered Fun* (The Lichfield Press, 2001), copyright © Celia Warren 2001, reprinted by permission of the author.

All other poems are published for the first time in this collection by permission of their authors:

Clare Bevan: 'Unicorn' and 'Pegasus', both copyright © Clare Bevan 2002; **Liz Brownlee:** 'Waiting', copyright © Liz Brownlee 2002; **Richard Caley:** 'Riddle', copyright © Richard Caley 2002; **Andrew Collett:** 'Before', copyright © Andrew Collett 2002; **Paul Cookson:** 'Trick or Treat' and 'Invisible Magicians', both copyright © Paul Cookson 2002; **Sue Cowling:** 'The Forest of No Return', copyright © Sue Cowling 2002; **Mary Green:** 'Charm Bracelet', copyright © Mary Green 2002; **Trevor Harvey:** 'Lost Magic', copyright © Trevor Harvey 2002; **Mike Johnson:** 'Advice to Young Wizards', copyright © Mike Johnson 2002; **Jean Kenward:** 'Troll', copyright © Jean Kenward 2002; **Tony Langham:** 'Spells'R'Us', copyright © Tony Langham 2002; **Granville Lawson:** 'Gypsy Rosa', copyright © Granville Lawson 2002; **Patricia Leighton:** 'Come In!', copyright © Patricia Leighton 2002; **Ann Logan:** 'Wishing Well', copyright © Ann Logan 2002; **Jenny Morris:** 'To Speak a Spell', copyright © Jenny Morris 2002; **Frances Nagle:** 'The Babysitter', copyright © Frances Nagle 2002; **Judith Nicholls:** 'Once...', copyright © Judith Nicholls 2002; **Marcus Parry:** 'Which Witch?', copyright © Marcus Parry 2002; **Gervase Phinn:** 'Tonight's the Night', copyright © Gervase Phinn 2002; **Rita Ray:** 'Wizard Witter World', copyright © Rita Ray 2002; **Cynthia Rider:** 'The Wizard' and 'Midsummer Magic' both copyright © Cynthia Rider 2002; **Roger Stevens:** 'The Brown Bear', copyright © Roger Stevens 2002; **Marian Swinger:** 'The Miserable Wizard of Misery Hall', 'The Wonderful Hat', and 'Thomas the Troll', all copyright © Marian Swinger 2002; **Angela Topping:** 'Midsummer Night', copyright © Angela Topping 2002; **Clive Webster:** 'Hokum Pokum', copyright © Clive Webster 2002; **David Whitehead:** 'The Witches' Under-World Cup Final', copyright © David Whitehead 2002; **Brenda Williams:** 'Sailor's Warning', copyright © Brenda Williams 2002; **Kate Williams:** 'Wicked Winter Tree', copyright © Kate Williams 2002.

Although we have tried to trace and contact the copyright holders before publication, in some cases this has not been possible. If contacted we will be pleased to rectify any errors or omissions at the earliest opportunity.